EVERYDAY
DISCIPLESHIP

7 ENCOUNTERS TO POINT
PEOPLE TO JESUS

DR. WARREN HAYNES

Everyday Discipleship, 7 Encounters to Point People to Jesus: A Companion to Discipleship Uncomplicated

Copyright © 2022 by Dr. Warren Haynes

Dr. Warren Haynes

A Companion to Discipleship Uncomplicated

READ THIS...

Just to say thanks for purchasing my book, I would like to give you the Group Guidebook 100% Free!

CLICK HERE TO DOWNLOAD

(or go to https://EverydayDiscipleship-GroupGuidebook.now.site)

| WELCOME

You've experienced moments that have taken your breath away. You've encountered people that have left an unforgettably good impression. You've heard words that have imprinted themselves in your thinking and motivated you to become more. During the next 7 days you will experience ways to create those moments, say those words, and be that person.

WELCOME to *Everyday Discipleship, 7 Encounters to Point People to Jesus!*

DEDICATION

This work is dedicated to the One who changed my destiny through a profoundly ordinary encounter. I also want to express my deepest gratitude to the countless disciples who followed the Holy Spirit's lead, stepped out in faith, and pointed me to Jesus. I will embrace you in eternity with gratitude and joy. Thank you!

> THEREFORE EVERYONE WHO HEARS THESE WORDS OF MINE AND PUTS THEM INTO PRACTICE IS LIKE A WISE MAN WHO BUILT HIS HOUSE ON THE ROCK.

MATTHEW 7:24

CONTENTS

INTRODUCTION

Jesus went about His days encountering people. He saw them, He healed them, He fed them, and He taught them. *(Explore Matthew 9:36, 14:14, 15:32, & Mark 6:34.)* Jesus brought hope and life to ordinary people in everyd ay situations and so can we. After all, He has breathed upon us His Holy Spirit and given us the commission to preach the Gospel throughout the world.

Often, our opportunities to spread the Good News are not going to take place in some far-flung field. It will usually look like an everyday occurrence, normal and not too exciting. But what may appear as happenstance can become an opportunity to experience a divine encounter. The goal of *Everyday Discipleship* is to demonstrate how you can develop a lifestyle that points people to Jesus.

Discipleship at its core should feel more like a conversation than a class.

Everyday Discipleship uses measured exposure to increase your disciple-making capacity. Each day you will read an encouraging story, complete a daily encounter, reflect on what you learned, and share insights with a friend. It's one thing to read about discipleship; it's another thing to experience what making disciples feels like in everyday moments.

Here are seven ways to maximize your *Everyday Discipleship* experience.

Follow this daily layout:

1. Get up in the morning. *That's the hard part!*
2. Pray.
3. Read the daily encouragement.
4. Complete the daily encounter.
5. Record a daily reflection.
6. Share insights with a friend.
7. Express gratitude to God and others.

Everyday Discipleship works best as a shared experience. Remember, Jesus did not minister by Himself. The disciples did not minister by themselves. They invited others to join them along the way. Discipleship is like a team sport; it is designed to be shared. These moments, conversations, and encounters we experience remind us of God's presence and fill us with His strength and purpose as we share them with one another. Here are seven ways your congregation or group can enhance their *Everyday Discipleship* experience.

Follow this weekly layout for groups:

1. Get organized, plan, and pray for an 8-day experience: A Sunday through Sunday schedule is optimal for congregations.

2. Pray, Pray, Pray and Communicate, Communicate, Communicate.

3. First Sunday: The sermon will set the basis and goal for the experience. (Explore Acts 8:26–40. Title: "One Encounter Can Change Everything.")

4. Find or assign partners: Make sure everyone has a friend to share insights with throughout the week. If insights are not being shared, discipleship isn't happening.

5. On Saturday: Organize small groups to complete the final encounter, share insights, and pray together. In homes with refreshments is ideal.

6. Second Sunday morning: Focus on Jesus, enjoy what He has done, and praise Him greatly. It's likely you will have guests, so focus on making this a positive, uplifting experience. They may want to come back next week. (Explore Matthew 4:18–23. Titles: "Following Jesus Changes Everything" or "The One Thing Every Disciple Must Do – Follow Jesus.")

7. Second Sunday evening: Have a corporate gathering with an open mic. Participants can share their encounters and insights.

If you would like to:

Share your experiences with me. I would love to hear them.

Request me to speak to your congregation or group. It would be my honor.

Use this book in any other way to promote discipleship and Christian growth.

Just ask. Here is my contact information:
https://ovou.me/whhaynes

Thank you for participating in *Everyday Discipleship, 7 Encounters to Point People to Jesus*! May the Lord Jesus fill you and make Himself known to you in new and profound ways.

Blessings,

Warren

SO WHETHER YOU EAT OR DRINK OR WHATEVER YOU DO, DO IT ALL FOR THE GLORY OF GOD.

EXPLORE 1 CORINTHIANS 10:31

DAY 1
WHAT WOULD HAPPEN?

PRAYER:

*Dear Jesus, teach me how to bring You glory
when I'm taking out the trash!*

DAY 1 – ENCOURAGEMENT

I began my ministry as the pastor of the First Baptist
Church of Dallas. Needless to say, the expectations were
high for this vastly inexperienced minister. Did I mention
it was the First Baptist church of Dallas... Oregon? Not
Dallas, Texas. I served as the pastor of a *non*-mega church
and wore many hats.

My wife and I drove a van to pick up children every
Sunday. We made bulletins, cleaned up after services,
painted the facilities, taught Sunday School, led Vacation

Bible School, worked on building projects, went to camp with the youth, and did anything else needing ministry muscle.

We had just completed a wonderful week of Vacation Bible School. I was the proud teacher of the second-grade class. My class was the largest, in fact; we had 17 second graders. There was not a single room in our little building that could contain 17 enthusiastic second graders, so we conducted our class outside. Every day I prayed for good weather and for the kids to stay in the circle and out of the streets.

We were so excited when several children put their faith in Jesus during those action-filled days. At the end of the week, my wife planned a fantastic VBS celebration: a baked potato dinner and pie auction to enjoy what God had done and raise money to send youth to summer camp. She called the event "Dud-Your-Spud" and it was a smashing success.

After a full week of Vacation Bible School and this fundraiser to top it all off, I was exhausted and ready to go home. Late that Saturday night, after everyone had left the building, I was conducting a final walkthrough to check the lights and thermostats. All the while, I was thinking, *I need to get up early and somehow present a message that I am immensely underprepared to deliver.*

During this walkthrough, I stepped into the kitchen. There, to my surprise, was a giant mess all over the kitchen floor. I was not happy. My mutterings ran something to the effect of, "May a flock of seagulls hover over whoever did this."

However, being in ministry, I knew how these things worked. The first person to come into the kitchen the next day would ask, "Who was the last person in the building?" That no-good pastor, that's who! "He's too good to clean up and he left this mess for us?" would be the next question.

I went from being tired and unhappy to straight-up mad.

So, I grabbed a broom and a dustpan and went to work. Grumbling under my breath with fuming strokes, I began to sweep the floor. The more I swept, the madder I got. Then I heard these words in my mind:

> *Warren, if you clean the floor like this, all you'll get is a clean floor, but if you do it for Me, everything will be different.*

Now I was conflicted. Do I hold on to being mad or do I do what God is wanting me to do? This is called a crisis of belief. Has a scenario like this ever happened to you? You know what God wants, but you don't feel like doing it. You'd rather hold on to your anger and resentment.

What we do in moments like this reveal what we truly believe about God.

I laid down the broom and dustpan, got down on my knees in the middle of a messy kitchen, and prayed, "Jesus, I'm sorry! I want to sweep this floor for You and nobody else." When I opened my eyes and got up, it was as though He had swept away the hurt, disappointment, and anger.

I felt the pleasure of God!

Then the words, *"This is my son, whom I love; with him I am well pleased"* came to mind. (Explore Matthew 3:17.) My strength was renewed and I experienced abiding peace and unexplainable joy in the middle of a mess. Jesus doesn't wait on the other side of your messes; He meets you in the middle of them and walks with you through them. And only He can sweep up and clean out the far-bigger messes that wait unseen in the heart.

This late-night experience taught me a lasting lesson: when you love Jesus, you can sweep a floor and feel His pleasure. *"Whatever you do, work at it with all your heart, as working for the Lord, not for men, since you know that you will receive an inheritance from the Lord as a reward. It is the Lord Christ you are serving."* (Explore Colossians 3:23–24.)

What would happen if we tackled every task as though Jesus was with us, and we were doing it for Him, and we were doing it because we loved Him?

Everyday tasks are opportunities to experience Jesus!

Day 1 – Encounter

Select a task no one wants to do. Then do it as an expression of your love to Jesus.

DAY 1 – REFLECTION

Describe your experience:

What did you learn?

BUT NOW, THIS IS WHAT THE LORD SAYS — HE WHO CREATED YOU, O JACOB, HE WHO FORMED YOU. O ISRAEL: 'FEAR NOT FOR I HAVE REDEEMED YOU; I HAVE SUMMONED YOU BY NAME; YOU ARE MINE.'

EXPLORE ISAIAH 43:1

DAY 2
I CANNOT FORGET YOU

Prayer:

Dear Jesus, thank You for creating me, forming me, redeeming me, and calling me by name. I belong to You! Help me remind someone today who they belong to!

DAY 2 – ENCOURAGEMENT

The room was buzzing after an energetic breakout session on the significance of getting to know your neighbors and learning people's names. Inevitably after a talk like this, participants approach with a common confession: "I'm not good at remembering names." I usually counter that comment with, "How much time do you spend working at remembering names?" Touché!

This is normally followed by an awkward silence and an "Ah-ha" moment. The recognition that it does take a little work and ingenuity to call people by name. And the more we work at it, the better we get.

To be fair, this dilemma is made worse by some level of social anxiety we all have as humans. A few of the top anxiety triggers we share are the fear of dying, the fear of public speaking, and the fear of talking to strangers. Pretty much in that order. So, it is legitimately stressful striking up a conversation with someone you don't know. Yet, God made us social creatures who long for connection. Getting to know the names of people in close proximity is an important part of igniting those connections.

After this particular session, three pastors approached me with a revelation. "We are ashamed to say this. All three of us live in the same neighborhood and we never knew it until tonight. When you had us get into groups and do the 'Describe your Neighbors Exercise,' we discovered we live very close to each other, in the same neighborhood." We all had a good laugh about this reality check that often hits too close to home.

Next in line was a woman who described how, for the past seven years, she had been going to a Subway to eat lunch.

For years she and the woman who always prepared her sandwich referred to each other as Hun, Love, or Darling instead of by name.

She was convicted that she didn't know the woman's name. Then she looked at me with a new sense of determination and said, "Tomorrow, I will know her name!" That captures the issue!

We get to know a person's name when we determine to do so.

On one occasion, I was flying from Ontario to Denver. I sat next to a young woman who was around the same age as my older daughters. She was a runner, a college student, and a fantastic conversationalist. Addie was studying psychology with an aim to become a speech pathologist. There is no doubt she will do well and empower many children with new linguistic confidence. In what seemed to be the blink of an eye, the landing message rang through the airplane cabin.

I took a pen out of my bag and scribbled her name and a verse on the palm of my hand. It read:

"ADDIE

ISA 49:16"

Then I said, "Addie, I want to remember you and our conversation. This is one of the ways I remember people's names." I showed her the palm of my hand. A bright smile stretched across her face as she gazed at her name and a verse reference scribbled in blue ink on a stranger's hand.

I asked if she was familiar with this verse. She shook her head, no. So, I described how this verse paints a scene where God's people felt like God had forsaken and forgotten them. However, to this the Lord replied,

> *"Could a mother forget a nursing child?"*
> *This is not possible because, "I cannot forget*
> *you, because I have engraved your name on*
> *the palm of my hand."*
>
> **(Explore Isaiah 49:14–16.)**

Addie responded, "That is beautiful."

I said, "Yes, it is." I then thanked her for a fantastic conversation and a quick flight. She returned the thanks and we went our separate ways. I believe God uses these moments to encourage us and to accomplish His good, pleasing, and perfect will. (Explore Romans 12:1–2.)

DAY 2 – ENCOUNTER

Learn someone's name today. Write their name and Isa. 49:16 in ink on the palm of your hand and let it naturally wear off.

DAY 2 – REFLECTION

Describe your experience:

_____

_____

_____

_____

_____

_____

_____

_____

_____

_____

_____

_____

_____

_____

_____

_____

_____

_____

_____

_____

_____

_____

What did you learn?

FOR WHERE TWO OR THREE COME TOGETHER IN MY NAME, THERE AM I WITH THEM.

EXPLORE MATTHEW 18:20

DAY 3
IT'S NOT OUR WORDS

Prayer:

Dear Jesus, thank You for being with me. Your presence rejuvenates me. Help me to bring someone into Your presence today!

DAY 3 – ENCOURAGEMENT

Traversing unfamiliar airports can be perplexing. I found myself trying to navigate a mass of humanity in the Atlanta airport. As I made my way toward my gate, I noticed a soldier outfitted in desert battle fatigues complete with a chock-full rucksack. Having served in the military, I have a great respect for the few and the brave. Men and women willing to put their lives on the line for others are worthy of gratitude.

This young man carrying the weight of war readiness on his back stopped for a moment to look at his ticket. People streamed by him on both sides as he stood like a rock holding its position in rushing water.

I approached him, established eye contact, and said, "Thank you for your service. I appreciate you."

He was quick to respond, "You're welcome."

Following this brief encounter, I continued toward my gate. As I was walking briskly to catch my own flight, I sensed the Spirit speaking to me.

That's not enough.

I didn't know what to do except to turn around and start walking back toward where I had spoken to him. It doesn't take long to lose sight of a person in a sea of people. However, as my gaze darted across the distance, I spotted the backpack and quickened my pace to catch him.

When I caught up with him, I still didn't know what I was supposed to do or say. So, I said, "Hey, there's no way for you to know this, but I am one of those preacher types." Looking back, it wasn't the smoothest way to enter a conversation. Nevertheless, God often does His best work through what little we bring to the table. Then I asked him where he was being deployed. With some calculated discretion, he revealed he was going to war. My heart was moved as I began to consider the gravity of possibilities in front of him.

Then I asked if he had a family. He smiled and his eyes smiled too as he said, "Yes, I have a wife and two daughters."

I took the plunge and asked, "Would it be okay if I prayed for you?" He nodded his head and indicated that it would be very much appreciated. So, I asked his name, put my hand on his shoulder, bowed my head, and began to call out to our Father.

In the middle of a sea of people in a busy airport, I asked God to protect him and watch over him. I asked the Lord to watch over his wife and daughters and bring them back together and to keep them whole. I asked our Rock and Redeemer to provide for this young man and his family and give them wisdom. After I ran out of words, my amen was joined by his.

He grabbed my hand and thanked me for taking the time to pray for him and his family. I told him it was my pleasure, and it was. After a final, "You take care," I turned and started back toward my gate. As I walked, love for this young man filled me. Love for his wife and two daughters, whom I may never meet, came upon me.

It is God's presence that makes prayer powerful.

"What other nation is so great as to have their gods near them the way the Lord our God is near us whenever we pray to him?" (Explore Deuteronomy 4:7.) It's not our words that make the difference; it's His presence. When we pray with another person, we are ushered into the presence of God. And in that moment, His presence can change anything.

DAY 3 – ENCOUNTER

Pray with someone today.

_____
_____
_____
_____
_____
_____
_____
_____
_____
_____
_____
_____
_____
_____
_____
_____
_____
_____
_____
_____
_____
_____
_____
_____
_____

DAY 3 – REFLECTION

Describe your experience:

What did you learn?

IN HIM WAS LIFE, AND THAT LIFE WAS THE LIGHT OF MEN. THE LIGHT SHINES IN THE DARKNESS, BUT THE DARKNESS HAS NOT UNDERSTOOD IT.

EXPLORE JOHN 1:4–5

DAY 4
THE NATURE OF LIGHT

Prayer:

Dear Jesus, Your life is the light of men. Help me to shine Your light into someone's life today!

DAY 4 – ENCOURAGEMENT

After a speaking engagement, I was invited to lunch with a pastor and his staff. While we were waiting for our food to be served, the older youth minister began to share a story about youth ministry "back in the day."

He said, "The things we used to do would get us fired for sure today." Then he began to describe how one time they had a "Texas Chainsaw" youth event in the gym. That certainly got our attention.

And not only ours. A man was walking past us in the restaurant and said, "I want to hear the rest of this story." So, he sat down and joined our table.

The youth minister continued to describe how they played the Texas Chainsaw horror movie while the youth were huddled together in a blacked-out gymnasium. During the movie, at the exact moment the villain started up his chainsaw to go to work, the back doors to the gym crashed open and the youth minister was dressed up like the maniac. He started up his own chainsaw.

"You should have seen those kids scatter," he said. I can only imagine.

As he shared his story of kids running and screaming for their lives at the Texas Chainsaw youth event, I thought to myself, *I would have made my own door.* The thought also crossed my mind that maybe he should have been fired for that lack of judgement. Needless to say, we enjoyed his story, filled the place with hardy laughter, and overall had a little too much fun in the restaurant.

It turned out the man who randomly joined our table to listen to the story was the managing owner of the restaurant. We will call him John. John was super nice and thanked us for allowing him to join the fun. While John was sharing with us a few challenges of being the managing owner, he said something that I had never personalized.

He divulged, "When people come into the restaurant and ask for the manager, they want something. And usually they want it for free."

I went to bed that night reflecting on our encounter with John. I felt like God wanted me to do something. So, I started praying for John that night. When I pray for people, I begin with what I call the 3-P's. I ask God to *Protect* them, *Provide* for them and give them wisdom, and I pray that they will *Personally* come to know Jesus better. (Explore John 17.)

The next day, I was sitting in a bookstore that shared the same parking lot with the restaurant John managed. I sensed Jesus wanting me to do something for John; I just didn't know what. So, I found a nice card and it came to me that the gift of coffee is always good. I purchased a coffee shop gift card and wrote John a note.

The handwritten note went something like this:

> *"John, I know when someone asks for the manager, they want something. But today, I want to give you something. Enjoy a cup of coffee or hot chocolate on me. And I also want you to know I am praying that God will protect you and your family, that He will provide for you and give you wisdom. And that you will come to know Jesus better and better."*

Your Friend,

Warren

I waited for the doors to the restaurant to open at 5 p.m. The hostess unlocked the doors, welcomed me in, and asked if she could help me. I asked if the manager was in and would it be possible to speak with him. Her eyes dropped as if she were thinking, *It's starting early tonight.* She pointed behind her and said, "He's at the bar."

I saw John talking with another gentleman. As I approached, John stood up and asked if he could help me. I said, "John, you may not remember me, but I was with the group you joined Sunday to listen to the story about the Texas Chainsaw youth event." A big smile crossed his face as he tilted his head back re-enjoying the moment.

I continued, "John, you mentioned that when someone comes here and asks for the manager, they want something. But tonight, I want to give you something." I handed him the sealed envelope and said, "I hope this gets your night off to a good start."

He thanked me and I turned around and walked out of the restaurant. After the encounter, I felt the Spirit's affirmation that I had been faithful in that moment.

The pleasure of God is a worthy pursuit!

Months later, I was telling this story in a church gathering to encourage people to be creative and find ways to engage others. After the service, a young lady approached me and said, "Brother Warren, you don't know the rest of that story. I work at that restaurant." I was like, *No Way!* She then explained how John showed the card and shared its contents with everyone who worked there. Then she said, "You don't know how much that meant to him."

John shared that little light—in the shape of a card with its contents etched out in barely legible chicken scratch—

with this young lady and other employees I will never meet.

Light by its very nature shines!

> *"You are the light of the world. A city on a hill cannot be hidden. Neither do people light a lamp and put it on its stand, and it gives light to everyone in the house. In the same way, let your light shine before men, that they may see your good deeds and praise your Father in heaven." (Explore Matthew 5:14–16.) The good we do out of love for God to benefit others becomes salt and light so others can taste and see God's goodness and give thanks.*

DAY 4 – ENCOUNTER

Ask God to show you someone you would've otherwise overlooked and do something good for them.

DAY 4 – REFLECTION

Describe your experience:

_____

_____

_____

_____

_____

_____

_____

_____

_____

_____

_____

_____

_____

_____

_____

_____

_____

_____

_____

_____

_____

_____

_____

_____

What did you learn?

> ## THEN HE SAID TO ALL OF THEM: 'IF ANYONE WOULD COME AFTER ME, HE MUST DENY HIMSELF AND TAKE UP HIS CROSS DAILY AND FOLLOW ME.

EXPLORE LUKE 9:23

DAY 5
HE DOESN'T KNOW

Prayer:

Dear Jesus, I want to come after You, deny myself, take up whatever cross You want me to carry today, and follow You!

DAY 5 – ENCOURAGEMENT

Some friends took me on an amazing outing near the famous Sydney Opera House while I was visiting Australia. I was excited to get out and take in this experience. The husband is a dynamic pastor, gifted musician, and solid Christian leader. His wife is a generous, fun, hardworking business professional who works in the financial sector of downtown Sydney.

During our stroll, I asked Hanna to share with me the story of how she came to follow Christ. She grew up in Singapore, in a traditional Asian family that focused on success as a supreme life goal. When Hanna was a young girl in grade school, a daring young friend invited her to go to a Christian church. This request was in contradiction to her family's tradition and religious practice.

Against better judgement, she decided to go to a Christian church service with her friend. That night, she sang new songs, met some new people, and heard for the first time how Jesus loved her and gave His life for her. The story of God's grace and sacrificial love filled her thoughts as she walked back home in the dark.

Hanna quietly made her way to her room hoping no one would find out where she had been. After she had shut the door and breathed a sigh of relief for getting home without incident, she couldn't stop thinking about Jesus.

Then the door was forcefully flung open and her older brother stood before her with a stick in his hand.

"I know what you did tonight. I know you went to the Christian church. You dishonored our family." As the hurtful words cascaded, the sharp blows of the stick quickly followed. Hanna raised her thin arm to protect her face and head. Her cries for him to stop blurred together with the cracks of the stick.

After he stopped, he told her to never dishonor her family by going to the Christian church again. Then the door slammed shut as she sat alone on the floor, her arm pulsing with pain and tears blurring her vision. Right then and there, through her pain and tears, Hanna called to Jesus. She said, "Jesus, I will follow you. He doesn't know how strong I am."

Hanna has been following Jesus ever since. Now she is married to an amazing man, and a grateful mother of three. She is a successful businesswoman and a leader in the church. To hear Hanna share her story of coming to faith in Jesus was breathtaking. Jesus is the One who peered through eternity, fixed His gaze on a spirited young girl, and gave her the desires of her heart. *"Let the redeemed of the Lord tell their story – those he redeemed from the hand of the foe."* (Explore Psalm 107:2.)

I am so thankful a part of Hanna's story now lives in me. I have mentally replayed this walk and our conversation many times and it is a gift that keeps giving.

The simple phrase, "Tell me about..." has unlocked countless treasures for me and it can do the same for you.

People's stories are like fingerprints. They are unique to each person. Get to know people's stories and opportunities to share your story will come naturally.

We live in a world of constant distraction. A cascade of white noise, screen time distractions, and our growing attention deficient make it challenging to genuinely take in someone else's story. Learn to ask people to share some of their story with you. Treat these moments as a sacred trust and thank them for allowing you to take part of their journey.

DAY 5 – ENCOUNTER

Ask someone to share a part of their story with you.
Simply asking "Tell me about..." can get you started.

DAY 4 – REFLECTION

Describe your experience:

_____

_____

_____

_____

_____

_____

_____

_____

_____

_____

_____

_____

_____

_____

_____

_____

_____

_____

_____

_____

_____

_____

What did you learn?

PHILIP FOUND NATHANAEL AND TOLD HIM, 'WE HAVE FOUND THE ONE MOSES WROTE ABOUT IN THE LAW, AND ABOUT WHOM THE PROPHETS ALSO WROTE —
JESUS OF NAZARETH, THE SON OF JOSEPH.'
'NAZARETH! CAN ANYTHING GOOD COME FROM THERE?' NATHANAEL ASKED.
'COME AND SEE,' SAID PHILIP.

EXPLORE JOHN 1:45–46

DAY 6
THE ASSIGNMENT

Prayer:

Dear Jesus, You are the one whom Moses and the prophets wrote about! Help me invite someone to come and experience You today.

DAY 6 – Encouragement

It's not often I get the opportunity to speak two Sundays in a row at the same place. However, the opportunity opened up and I was excited to see what God might do. As I prayed and planned for this encounter, I contemplated a worthy experiment for the believers who would gather.

So, I decided the first week I would share a message focused on how Jesus gave personal invitations to move people to deeper levels of faith and relationship and how we can do the same. Then I would give the people an assignment to render a personal invitation to another person before the next Sunday.

The book of Matthew provides one of Jesus' first personal invitations.

"As Jesus was walking beside the Sea of Galilee he saw two brothers, Simon called Peter and his brother Andrew. They were casting a net into the lake, for they were fishermen. 'Come, follow me,' Jesus said, 'and I will make you fishers of men.' At once they left their nets and followed him."

Explore Matthew 4:18–20.

We can reflect on a few observations in this passage.

First, Jesus demonstrated that opportunities to impact others naturally unfold as we go through our day. *"As Jesus was walking..."* More often than not, we do not have to go out of our way to influence others. However, it's important to note these opportunities are cloaked in the ordinary. As such, they often go unnoticed. It's as we are walking, sitting, going, eating, working, etc., that influence is sown.

Second, what caused Jesus to see these two men? *"As Jesus was walking... he saw two men."* What causes us to really see people? How easy is it to walk by people you don't know versus how hard it is to walk by someone you know well without acknowledging them?

Here is an insightful comparative passage that helped me process the essence of connection: *"When Jesus saw the crowds, He had compassion on them..."* (Explore Matthew 9:36.) Compassion causes us to see people we would normally overlook.

The third observation I noticed was Jesus gave the two men a personal invitation. *"Come, follow me..."* The primary invitation Jesus offers to all of us is to a personal relationship. Consider how Jesus describes eternal life: *"Now this is eternal life: that they may know you, the only true God, and Jesus Christ, whom you have sent."* (Explore John 17:3.)

The invitation to eternal life is not to a place called Heaven; it's an invitation to enter into a relationship with Jesus. Through relationship with Jesus, all of God's promises become possible. *"For no matter how many promises God has made, they are 'Yes' in Christ."*

(Explore 2 Corinthians 1:20.) Jesus invites us to an eternal personal relationship.

This leads to the final observation. As Peter and Andrew followed Jesus, Jesus would make them into what they could not become without Him. *"...and I will make you fishers of men."* When Jesus calls you, He sees what you can be. He stands ready to develop you into more than you currently think possible. There is a deep potential in every person that can only be realized in relationship with Jesus.

Do you remember the Bible passage in which Jesus told Peter and the other fishermen to cast their nets again after a long night of unproductive fishing? Though reluctant, they cast the nets once more and caught so many fish the nets started to break and the boats began to sink. (Explore Luke 5:1–11.)

Now, fast forward to the time Peter, "the fisher of men," stood before the crowd on Pentecost and delivered a message that inspired thousands of people to believe in Jesus, repent of personal sins, be baptized, and become a part of God's family. (Explore Acts 2:14–41.)

Peter had no idea what he was capable of, but Jesus did! Never underestimate the power of a personal invitation. Take a moment to reflect on an invitation that influenced you to love Jesus and develop beyond what you thought possible.

After I shared these observations in church that first Sunday, I gave the congregation the assignment for the following week. I suggested that they call the person by name and look in their eyes and say something like, "Ben or Sally, would you come to church with me this Sunday?" The words "with me" are what transform this from a general invitation to a personal invitation. Jesus modeled this with Peter and Andrew.

I explained the ultimate goal was not to get people to a building, but to develop a Christ-honoring personal relationship with them.

> *"To them God has chosen to make known among the Gentiles the glorious riches of this mystery, which is Christ in you, the hope of glory."*

Explore Colossians 1:27.

As they get to know us, we help them get to know Jesus.

I reminded the audience I would ask them the following week about the challenge and who had personally invited someone to share a church experience with them. The next Sunday rolled around and I knew right away not many had completed the assignment. The congregation looked very similar to the week prior.

However, I ventured ahead and asked those gathered who had remembered the assignment from last week. A quick, *Oh Snap!* went across the congregation like the Wave at a sporting event. *He remembered!* Then I asked, "Did anyone give a personal invitation to someone this week? Did you call them by name, look them in the eyes and say something like, 'Would you come to church with me this Sunday?' And if so, what happened?"

I quickly surveyed the auditorium and two hands shot up. Two women with glowing faces and hands lifted high. Both women had people sitting next to them. One had brought two friends and the other had brought three. Both women exuded genuine excitement for their friends and they also displayed a confidence that comes from a growing faith.

While the rest of the congregation looked as though they were hoping this moment would pass a little quicker, the moment slowed down for me as I looked across the congregation and saw the two who were willing to do the work. Then the Spirit brought these words to mind: *"The harvest is plentiful, but the workers are few."* (Explore Matthew 9:37–38.)

Jesus said, *"The harvest is plentiful."* This is present tense. The harvest is always plentiful. This is a statement of fact. The truth of the harvest is that it is plentiful. The problem with this plentiful harvest is this: there are only a few workers. Only a few are willing to do the work. This experience reminds me to get in the field and get to work.

The harvest is still plentiful; it's the workers who are few.

DAY 6 – ENCOUNTER

Make eye contact, call someone by name, and ask, "Would you come to church *with me* this Sunday?"

_____

_____

_____

_____

_____

_____

_____

_____

_____

_____

_____

_____

_____

_____

_____

_____

_____

_____

_____

DAY 4 – REFLECTION

Describe your experience:

What did you learn?

_____

_____

_____

_____

_____

_____

_____

_____

_____

_____

_____

_____

_____

_____

_____

_____

_____

_____

_____

_____

THEY BROKE BREAD IN THEIR HOMES AND ATE TOGETHER WITH GLAD AND SINCERE HEARTS, PRAISING GOD AND ENJOYING THE FAVOR OF ALL THE PEOPLE.

EXPLORE ACTS 2:46

DAY 7
THIS SHOULD BE NORMAL

Prayer:

Dear Jesus, thank You for other believers. May I encourage others to follow You closer and love You more.

DAY 7 – ENCOURAGEMENT

Following a challenging martial arts training session, the participants were invited to stay for Bible study and lunch. The coaches shared how they came to follow Jesus and what a difference He had made in their lives. Then the pastor stood and delivered a clear and compelling gospel presentation.

It was a fantastic Good News gathering in a seemingly unlikely setting. It was a beautiful and pure moment. There was no pretense or forced messaging, only authentic, unhindered, heartfelt expressions of faith. To say I was encouraged would be a significant understatement.

Every time we gather is an opportunity to sow seeds of faith, to encourage, and to build others up. While enjoying some superb tacos after the meeting, a group of students gathered around a table to eat and socialize. I initiated some small-talk with the young man sitting next to me and learned a little more about his journey. He mentioned he had tried reading the Bible, but barely made it past Genesis.

I responded, "I get that! Many people struggle reading the Bible. One thing to consider when approaching the Bible is you can't read it like you read other books. We often read books to get information or to learn something. Reading the Bible requires a different approach. Imagine someone you love deeply sends you a handwritten letter. What would you do with it? Would you read it and throw it away?"

I continued, "My dad wrote me a seven-page letter when I graduated college. Where do you think that letter is today?... It's in a safe! Because that is how you handle words from someone you love. You treasure them because they are precious to you. That is how we are to approach reading the Bible. As words written to us from someone we love deeply and who loves us beyond measure."

He said, "That makes a lot of sense. I never thought of it like that before." Others sitting at the table, who had been listening, chimed in with appreciation for helping them understand the Bible better. Then a young woman shared how she had recently come to faith in Jesus and expressed how she wanted to become a better follower. Overall, it felt like we shared a conversation that mattered.

Discipleship should feel and look more like these moments. This is what Jesus did. As He went, He had conversations. And later, He and the disciples talked about those encounters and what they needed to know. Gathering with people talking about Jesus and encouraging one another to live as His followers should be normal. There is a passage that captures this everyday discipleship picture perfectly:

"They devoted themselves to the apostles' teaching and to the fellowship, to the breaking of bread and to prayer. Everyone was filled with awe, and many wonders and miraculous signs were done by the apostles.

All the believers were together and had everything in common. Selling their possessions and goods, they gave to anyone as had need. Every day they continued to meet together in the temple courts. They broke bread in their homes and ate together with glad and sincere hearts, praising God and enjoying the favor of all the people. And the Lord added to their number daily those who were being saved."

Explore Acts 2:42–47.

DAY 7 – ENCOUNTER

Host or join a small group in someone's home. Share a meal, pray, and share your encounters and insights to encourage one another.

_____

_____

_____

_____

_____

_____

_____

_____

_____

_____

_____

_____

_____

_____

_____

_____

_____

_____

_____

_____

_____

DAY 7 – REFLECTION

Describe your experience:

_____

_____

_____

_____

_____

_____

_____

_____

_____

_____

_____

_____

_____

_____

_____

_____

_____

_____

_____

_____

What did you learn?

| CONCLUSION

Thank you for participating in *Everyday Discipleship, 7 Encounters to Point People to Jesus*. Discipleship was never meant to be something we do once a week. It was always meant to be an everyday way of life.

Here is a quick day-to-day recap of this week.

> ➢ **Day one,** you learned to cultivate a good heart by doing undesirable tasks out of love for Jesus.

> ➢ **Day two,** you practiced the importance of remembering names by writing a name on the palm of your hand.

> ➢ **Day three,** you brought someone into the presence of God when you prayed with them.

> ➢ **Day four,** you spread salt and light so others could taste and see the goodness of God.

➤ **Day five,** you valued taking a genuine interest in someone by listening to their story.

➤ **Day six,** you gave a powerful and personal invitation to move someone to take the next step in their journey.

➤ **Day seven,** you gathered with other believers to strengthen and encourage one another.

That is a fantastic week!

Every day you created encounters, in partnership with the Holy Spirit, to point people to Jesus. Don't stop! Keep up the good work because this world needs you to help them get to Jesus. It is my sincere hope that taking the steps outlined in this book drew you closer to Jesus, made you more in tune to the Spirit's leading, and brought you closer to other believers.

May the Lord bless you as you continue to point people to Jesus!

GROUP GUIDE

Don't forget your FREE Group Guidebook!

CLICK HERE TO DOWNLOAD

(or go to https://EverydayDiscipleship-GroupGuidebook.now.site)

If you would like to:

- ➢ Share your experiences with me. I would love to hear them!
- ➢ Request me to speak to your congregation or group, it would be my honor.
- ➢ Use this book in any other way.

Just ask. Here is my contact info:
https://ovou.me/whhaynes

Thank you for participating in *Everyday Discipleship, 7 Encounters to Point People to Jesus*! May the Lord Jesus fill you and make Himself known to you in new and profound ways.

Blessings,

Warren

ABOUT THE AUTHOR

Warren Haynes is the director of the *ADVANCE* program for Gateway Seminary and author of *Everyday Discipleship*. He is known for his Keynote Addresses, "Love God, Love People," "Release Compassion," and "Make Conversations Matter." Warren's books, courses, and conferences on *Discipleship Uncomplicated*, *Release Compassion*, *Everyday Discipleship*, and *How to Communicate on Purpose* inspire Christians worldwide.

Warren holds a Doctor of Ministry degree in the area of Dialogue and serves on faculty at Gateway Seminary. He brings a refreshing and insightful approach to interacting and influencing people. He enjoys roasting coffee, adventuring, trying new foods, partaking in inspired conversations, and doing life with his wife and four children.

OTHER BOOKS BY DR. HAYNES

Discipleship Uncomplicated is intensely practical and easy to follow!

It takes the guesswork out of getting started and provides exactly what you need to know and do to start making disciples.

Whether you are an introverted wallflower or an over-the-top people person, *Discipleship Uncomplicated* delivers **exactly what you need** to start **influencing people for**

Jesus. Here are some of the **powerful principles** and **practices** you will discover:

➢ How to **pinpoint the people** you are most likely to influence for Jesus

➢ How to bring **spiritual power** into your personal relationships

➢ How to **create** relational **breakthroughs**

➢ How to build **strong** relational **connections**

➢ How to **move people spiritually**

➢ How to **gather** and **influence people** to follow Jesus

➢ How to **multiply leaders** and reach **new** people

https://www.youtube.com/watch?v=JBB052guOyk&t=14s

How to Communicate on Purpose, 12 Skills Christians Need to Make Conversations Matter

Improve your Conversations, Improve your Life!

Imagine having the skills to navigate challenges and inspire others with purpose, precision, and confidence. Now you can. Dr. Warren Haynes uses his relatable style, biblical knowledge, and storytelling to introduce 12 incredible conversation skills.

You'll learn how to...

> **Deal with fear** and increase your capacity

> **Respond appropriately** to conversations

> **Keep your thoughts in line** and engage others

> Display and **detect authenticity**

> Enter, expand, and exit **conversations with grace**

> **Capture insights** from past conversations to use in future ones

> **Share stories** to grow wisdom and relationships

> **Build rapport** with almost anyone

> **Explore opportunities** that lead to beneficial discoveries

> **Find root problems** and pressure-test ideas

> **Craft** win-win agreements

> **Prevail with logic and love**

https://www.youtube.com/watch?v=MbRFxI9jG2M&t=16s

Made in the USA
Las Vegas, NV
07 May 2023

71706591R00049